Waiting i

Daily

Advent and

Year A

Jay Cormier

LITURGICAL PRESS

Collegeville, Minnesota

www.litpress.org

Nihil Obstat: Rev. Robert C. Harren, J.C.L., *Censor deputatus.*

Imprimatur: ✠ Most Rev. John F. Kinney, J.C.D., D.D., Bishop of St. Cloud, February 22, 2007.

Cover design by Ann Blattner.

ISSN 1550-803X

ISBN: 978-0-8146-3080-8

Introduction

"The grace of God has appeared . . . !"

The apostle Paul wrote these simple words of extraordinary hope to his beloved coworker Titus. For Paul, this grace is not simply a beautiful but vague theological theory; rather, it is the Spirit of God enabling us to live the justice and compassion of the gospel of Jesus, the Risen One who continues to live in the midst of God's people.

"We live always during Advent," Jean Danielou wrote. "We are always waiting for the Messiah to come. The Messiah has come, but is not yet fully manifest. The Messiah is not fully manifest in each of our souls, not fully manifest in humankind as a whole: that is to say, that as Christ was born according to the flesh in Bethlehem of Judah, so must he be born according to the spirit in each of our souls."

Giving birth to Christ. As we go about our lives, we sense a certain inconclusiveness and incompleteness; we have much to do and complete in our time on earth; there is much to make right and whole in our lives. Fear, fulfillment, expectation, hope, and anxiety are all part of the Advent experience every one of us lives. The Messiah Jesus, God's love and grace made flesh, comes to complete, to fulfill, to heal, to liberate. He is Emmanuel—"God is with us." These days of Advent and Christmas call us to "behold" God in our midst, to give birth to his love and justice in our own stables.

The stories and reflections included in this year's edition of *Waiting in Joyful Hope* all point to the "grace of God" in our midst. Within our families and classrooms, our workplaces and playgrounds, the love of God is present; in every relationship, in every decision, in every conflict, the Spirit of God moves and prompts us to what is right and just.

May the pages that follow help make these days of Advent waiting and Christmas joy a time for rediscovering the ever-faithful God in your midst. And may that presence be born again and again in every day of every season of the New Year.

FIRST WEEK OF ADVENT

December 2: First Sunday of Advent

A Promise Not Kept

Readings: Isa 2:1-5; Rom 13:11-14; Matt 24:37-44

Scripture:
". . . stay awake!
For you do not know on which day your Lord will come."
(Matt 24:42)

Reflection: On Christmas morning 2003, author Joan Didion's only daughter fell into septic shock from a runaway pneumonia infection. Five days later, after returning home from the hospital to visit their daughter, Didion's husband, writer John Gregory Dunne, slumped over in his chair. He died an hour later as the result of a massive heart attack.

Didion's extraordinary book, *The Year of Magical Thinking*, chronicles her dealing with the death of her husband and the critical illness of her daughter Quintana (who died at the age of 39). Didion recounts a particularly touching moment that occurred only months after her husband's death. Quintana had just been released from a New York hospital. Her husband Gerry took her to Malibu to recuperate, but Quintana became ill during the flight. Upon landing she was rushed to the UCLA Medical Center and underwent emergency neurosurgery. Joan rushed to California to be with her daughter. Quintana was breathing through a tube in her throat; she was heavily medicated.

Seeing her mother, Quintana struggled to speak, "When do you have to leave?"

"When we can leave together," her mother said. "You're safe. I'm here. You're going to be all right."

Quintana's face relaxed and she went back to sleep.

Joan Didion writes about that moment:

"It occurred to me during those weeks that this had been, since the day we brought her home from [the hospital], my basic promise to her. I would not leave. I would take care of her. . . . It also occurred to me that this was a promise that I could not keep. I could not always take care of her. I could not never leave her. She was no longer a child. She was an adult. Things happen that mothers could not prevent or fix."

Didion's *Year of Magical Thinking* is the story of her own Advent, when she was forced to confront change, illness, and death. Her experience mirrors the Advents we all experience: the realization that our time is precious and limited, that our lives constantly change and turn and are transformed. The season of Advent we begin today calls us to "think magically" to understand the purpose of life in the midst of illness and death. Advent challenges us to "stay awake" and "watch" for the signs of God's unmistakable presence in our lives, to live our lives as a gift from God.

Meditation: In what experiences have you become aware of the preciousness of time and the fragility of life?

Prayer: Come, Lord, into the Advent of our lives. Come, open our eyes to see your hand in all things. Come, illuminate the paths we walk as we journey to your dwelling place.

To Wait in Hope

Readings: Isa 4:2-6; Matt 8:5-11

Scripture:
The centurion said [to Jesus] in reply,
"Lord, I am not worthy to have you enter under my roof;
only say the word and my servant will be healed." (Matt 8:8)

Reflection: When we're sick, it's usually just a matter of time. Our joints are aching, our heads are pounding, our stomachs have declared war on us—but we know that it's only a matter of waiting out the cold or flu. In time, we know we'll be feeling better.

Then there are times when the waiting is more uncertain, more anxious, more desperate. We wait for the lab results, we wait to see if the medicine will work, we wait for the surgery to be completed, we wait for a cure.

And sometimes we are left waiting—sometimes we're not sure exactly what we're waiting for or how and when we will know that our waiting is at an end. We wait for the prodigal child to come to his or her senses and come home, we wait for the conflict to be resolved and tension to end, we wait for something good to come our way. We wait for resolution, we wait for something new, we wait for some reason to hope.

Waiting for healing, waiting for restoration, waiting for something new and better is the season of Advent. The centurion in today's gospel is the model of Advent waiting. With patient and generous care, he has waited through his servant's illness. His faith enables him to dare to hope that his and his seriously ill servant's waiting will be brought to completion in this Jesus. With a rare combination of dignity and humility, he asks Jesus to speak a word of healing.

This season of Advent calls us to hope that our waiting, our yearning for healing, for peace, for salvation, will come in God's good time.

Meditation: How is your life an Advent experience of waiting? In what ways do you feel your life is "incomplete"? What voids in your life have you discovered can be filled only by God?

Prayer: O Christ, healer and worker of wonders, be with us in our waiting. May we trust in your word to heal our afflictions and illnesses; may we hope in your light to shatter the darkness of our despair and pain. Let us live the Advent of our lives with faith in your compassion and hope in your grace.

December 4: Tuesday of the First Week of Advent

What Would the Rabbi See Today?

Readings: Isa 11:1-10; Luke 10:21-24

Scripture:

". . . many prophets and kings desired to see what you see,
but did not see it,
and to hear what you hear, but did not hear it." (Luke 10:24)

Reflection: Martin Buber, the great Jewish philosopher and mystic, delighted in telling the story of a revered rabbi in Jerusalem. One day, a young student of the rabbi came running into the rabbi's study.

"Rabbi, Rabbi! It's true! The Messiah has finally come!" the student announced.

The rabbi calmly rose from his chair and walked over to the window. He looked carefully up and down the street. He then said to his excited friend that nothing seemed to have changed, and he quietly returned to his work.

If the rabbi in Buber's story were to look out of his window during our celebration of the Messiah's birth, he would certainly experience many different things: he would see lights and decorations and greenery, he would hear the songs of "joy to the world" and "peace on earth," he would be greeted with smiles and good wishes. But what would the rabbi see out of his window on December 26 or January 17 or in late February or on a hot day next July?

But the Messiah has come! What happened on that Palestinian night when a son was born to a carpenter and his young bride was a watershed moment in the history of humanity, the first light of a new morning for all men and women of goodwill. But has the Messiah's coming made a difference? Has our world become a better place since the Son of God walked among us? Has anything changed?

May Christ's coming this Christmas be the beginning of a profound difference in our homes and hearts, transforming our attitudes and perspectives in the compassion and mercy of God.

Meditation: How would your life be different had Christ *not* come?

Prayer: God of compassion, may our prayerful observance of this Advent season be the beginning of a profound difference in our homes and hearts. May the dawning of your Christ be a new day of justice for all who are oppressed and rejected; may his coming usher in an eternal day of peace among all nations and peoples.

The Blessings of Sharing

Readings: Isa 25:6-10a; Matt 15:29-37

Scripture:

Then he took the seven loaves and the fish,
gave thanks, broke the loaves,
and gave them to the disciples, who in turn gave them
to the crowds.
They all ate and were satisfied. (Matt 15:36-37)

Reflection: A poor woman carrying a small pail came to Mother Teresa's soup kitchen to beg for rice for her children. Mother Teresa took her small pail and filled it with rice from the kitchen's bin. After thanking Mother for her kindness, the woman took out a second container and poured half of the rice into it.

"Why did she do that?" Mother Teresa was asked. She explained that the second container was for another family near the woman's home who could not make the long trek to the soup kitchen. Mother Teresa was asked why, then, did she not offer to fill the second container for the woman.

Mother Teresa answered, "Because I did not want to deprive her of the blessing of sharing."

The miracle recounted in today's gospel is a miracle about sharing. When confronted with the needs of the crowds, Jesus takes all that the apostles have managed to collect—

seven loaves of bread and a few fish, according to Matthew's version—and feeds everyone.

This story—the only miracle of Jesus recounted in all four gospels—was especially cherished by the early church: the first generations of Christians saw in Jesus' feeding of the crowds a precursor to the Eucharist (notice the four verbs: "*took* bread," "*gave* thanks," "*broke*," "*gave*"—the same four verbs that describe Jesus' actions at the Last Supper). It is a wonderful gospel to pray over as we begin this season of sharing and gift giving. Advent anticipates God's greatest gift to his people—the gift of himself in the person of Christ. At our parish table, we celebrate that gift in the simple blessings of bread and wine. All that God asks of us is that we be willing to become bread and wine—Eucharist—for one another.

Meditation: How can you become Eucharist for someone this Christmas? What can you "take" from your own needs and wants, "bless" in the compassion of God, "break" from your own poverty, and "give" so that others may "eat"?

Prayer: O Christ, Bread of Life and Living Water come down from heaven, you give yourself to us with complete joy and total love. May our Christmas giving this year reflect that joy and love. Take the pieces of bread and fish that we are able to give and transform them into vehicles of your compassion for those we love. Let our generosity and giving in every season be, for us, blessings of sharing.

Christmas Wish List

Readings: Isa 26:1-6; Matt 7:21, 24-27

Scripture:

"Everyone who listens to these words of mine and acts on them
will be like the wise man who built his house on rock." (Matt 7:24)

Reflection: It is a pre-Christmas staple in newspapers and on many local television news shows: asking people, especially celebrities, *What's the best Christmas present you ever received?*

Most of us have special memories of finding something under the tree on Christmas morning that has made us especially happy, something that brought a lasting joy to our hearts, maybe even something that changed our lives.

But have you ever thought about the best present you ever *gave?* It was probably something you put a great deal of thought into, not only thinking of the gift itself, but also of the person receiving it. Your gift also demanded more time, more effort—and, yes, probably more money—than you had planned. But when you gave it, you could sense immediately that you had touched the receiver deeply, that the receiver realized all that you put into the gift. Your gift may have even changed or transformed the receiver's life.

And you felt more joy over giving the gift than had you received the gift yourself.

Such an attitude of gift giving is not only the true spirit of Christmas but also the essence of the gospel call to love one another as Christ has loved us—love that is the "rock" on which Christ calls us to build our lives: love that finds its joy in bringing joy to another; love that helps us struggle through the storms that batter us every day; love that sees and welcomes Christ in every heart.

Meditation: What is the best gift that you can give someone you love this Christmas?

Prayer: O God, may your Spirit of compassion and forgiveness open our hearts to hear you in the voices of one another and see you in the struggles of those around us; may your Spirit unclench our hands and unlock our souls so we may give to others as you have given to us, that we may forgive as you have forgiven us, that we may lift one another up in our life's journey as you lift us up to the place where you dwell.

"All heal"

Readings: Isa 29:17-24; Matt 9:27-31

Scripture:

When he entered the house,
the blind men approached him and Jesus said to them,
"Do you believe I can do this?"
"Yes, Lord," they said to him.
Then he touched their eyes and said,
"Let it be done for you according to your faith." (Matt 9:28-29)

Reflection: Many of our homes will be decorated this Christmas with sprigs of mistletoe. But there's more to the custom than just stealing a kiss from your beloved.

The druids of pre-Christian times considered mistletoe sacred. Every year at the winter solstice druid priests would solemnly cut down mistletoe branches and distribute them among the people, who would then hang sprigs of mistletoe over their doors, believing that the powers of the plant would protect their homes from thunder, lightning, and every sort of evil.

The English called mistletoe "all heal." Mistletoe, a parasite that grows on oak trees, was a popular folk remedy used by herbalists to make a salve for treating any number of maladies, including toothaches, measles, and dog bites. The

English also believed that wearing mistletoe around their necks would protect them from the power of devils and witches.

The tradition of kissing under mistletoe has been traced to a number of legends. According to a Viking myth, Frigga, the goddess of love, saved her son from the poison of mistletoe by removing the plant's toxin with her tears. When her son came back to life, Frigga, out of happiness and gratitude, kissed everyone who passed underneath mistletoe.

The mistletoe plant was adopted by the Christian church as a symbol of Christ the Divine Healer, who restored sight to the blind, raised the dead to life, and preached good news to the poor. The mistletoe of our Christmas array reminds us that this is the season of healing: a time for bridging the divisions between ourselves and family and friends, a time for embracing the Messiah's selfless spirit of reconciliation and forgiveness, a time for restoring the love and peace of Christ within our hearts and homes.

Meditation: How can you bring healing and restoration into this Advent season through mending a broken or strained relationship?

Prayer: Christ the Healer, come into our hearts and homes this Advent season. Open our eyes with the light of your compassion, heal our hurts with your forgiveness, mend our brokenness with your peace.

December 8: Solemnity of the Immaculate Conception
(Catholic Church)

Saturday of the First Week of Advent
(Episcopal Church)

Yes!

Readings: Gen 3:9-15, 20; Eph 1:3-6, 11-12; Luke 1:26-38

Scripture:
". . . Behold, I am the handmaid of the Lord.
May it be done to me according to your word." (Luke 1:38)

Reflection: Great things begin with a simple, single word: *Yes*. A couple begins a new life together when they say *yes* to each other's promise of love and faithfulness; a doctor brings hope and healing to a poor South American village when she says *yes* to the opportunity to spend two weeks each year among the world's most destitute; a scientist's exhausting research leads him to break through the unknown and discover the *yes* of a new cancer drug, the *yes* of a more powerful microchip, the *yes* of the next generation of spacecraft.

Today, we celebrate Mary's *yes* to God's call to be what the church calls *Theotokos*—the "bearer of God." Despite her understandable confusion and fear, Mary's *yes* is offered in complete faith and trust in the God of all that is good. And because of her *yes*, so begins the new Genesis: the Christ event. In her *yes* to God, Mary our sister becomes a model and inspiration for our *yes* to God.

Our *yes* to God, though under far less extraordinary circumstances than Mary's, requires the same faith and trust. Every one of us is called to be "bearers of God" to our own small corners of the world. By God's grace, we are able to say *yes*—a *yes* that is total and committed, a *yes* that is selfless and giving, a *yes* that is clear and determined, a *yes* that is aware of the obstacles but sees reason for hope.

Meditation: What was the most important *yes* you have ever given? What causes you to be reluctant in giving your complete and trusting *yes* to the call of God?

Prayer: Gracious God, may we have the faith and trust of your daughter Mary to say *yes* to your call to be your presence in our own time and place. May our hearts say *yes* to the gift of your Son; may our spirits say *yes* to your invitation to bring that gift to our Advent world.

SECOND WEEK OF ADVENT

Rostrevor

Readings: Isa 11:1-10; Rom 15:4-9; Matt 3:1-12

Scripture:

John the Baptist appeared, preaching in the desert of Judea and saying, "Repent, for the kingdom of heaven is at hand!"

It was of him that the prophet Isaiah had spoken when he said:

A voice of one crying in the desert,
Prepare the way of the Lord,
make straight his paths. (Matt 3:1-3)

Reflection: In the midst of the hatred and violence that mars Northern Ireland, a community of five monks goes about a quiet life of prayer. Though low-key and unassuming, they have not gone unnoticed. The Benedictines of Holy Cross Monastery offer the people of Rostrevor in County Down a place of peace and a sanctuary from their troubles.

The monastery was established in 1998 by the French abbey of Bec, in response to a call by Benedictine abbeys to establish new foundations in places where Christians were having difficulty living side by side. Their mission is simple: to live the gospel according to the Rule of St. Benedict among Christians of different confessions. They are a living witness of Christ's compassion in a land stained by the blood of

Catholics and Protestants; their life of simple peace is a powerful prophecy in the face of violence and hatred. The small monastery welcomes Christians of every denomination. The monks also travel to Protestant churches to sing the Liturgy of the Hours. Villagers who had never spoken to one another have found themselves praying side by side in the monastery church.

Most of us have no idea of what it is like to live in a place where people are isolated from one another by a chasm of distrust and hatred that goes back generations. But in their simple living of the gospel, the monks of Rostrevor are trying to reverse attitudes and suspicions deeply ingrained in the Northern Irish psyche.

As the monks of Rostrevor are witnesses of Christ's peace in the midst of a people broken by sectarian violence, as John the Baptist proclaimed the coming of the Messiah in the austerity of his life and the baptism he offered, we are called by God to be prophets in our own place and time, to mirror, in our own often small, quiet ways, the reign of God in our midst.

Meditation: What simple everyday part of your life might be a small but authentic proclamation of the love of God to and for others?

Prayer: Come, Lord Jesus, restore our land and re-create our hearts. May we speak your word to those whose hearts have been hardened by despair and disappointment; may we create for you a highway of peace and reconciliation that passes through every heart and home.

"Roofer" Friends

Readings: Isa 35:1-10; Luke 5:17-26

Scripture:

But not finding a way to bring him in because of the crowd,
they went up on the roof
and lowered him on the stretcher through the tiles
into the middle in front of Jesus. (Luke 5:19)

Reflection: Consider the logistics: First, they had to carry their friend on a stretcher and maneuver their way through the unyielding crowds who wanted to see Jesus. When that didn't work, they devised a bold plan: they carefully hoisted their friend up on the roof of the house (probably up a flight of stairs outside the building, typical of Palestinian houses of the time), pushed aside the thatch and tiles, and gently lowered their friend, placing him directly in front of Jesus. It must have been quite a sight, which was probably met first with stunned silence by the onlookers, then by vehement protests at this man's bypassing the crowds. But his friends would not be dissuaded.

Such extraordinary love for another human being. Jesus could not have healed the paralyzed man if the man's friends—the "roofers"—had not been involved. Concern for their friend and confidence in Jesus' compassion compelled them to put all their ingenuity and muscle into bringing their paralyzed friend to Jesus the healer.

The "roofers" of today's gospel teach us what friendship—Christlike friendship—is all about: Friends who do not get stuck in self-interest and status but find joy in lifting one another up. Friends who are the first to pick up another's mat and carry another when he or she is wounded and broken—without having to be asked. Friends who readily offer all that they have—and readily accept those gifts from others with joy and gratitude. Friends who stand with one another at both their crosses and resurrections.

At this time of year, we are especially aware of the gift of friends—those individuals who have traveled the miles with us, offering their compassion and support, seeking nothing in return. In the gift of good friends we come to meet Jesus the healer and reconciler.

Meditation: Who are those friends of yours who, for you, would go so far as the "roofers" did for their paralyzed friend in Luke's Gospel? For whom are you a "roofer" friend?

Prayer: Help us, O God, to be sources of comfort and support, understanding and forgiveness for others, and may we discover, in the gift of our friends, the blessings of your grace.

My Shepherd Is My D.R.E.

Readings: Isa 40:1-11; Matt 18:12-14

Scripture:
"If a man has a hundred sheep and one of them goes astray,
will he not leave the ninety-nine in the hills
and go in search of the stray?" (Matt 18:12)

Reflection: Every parish director of religious education (D.R.E.) has had to deal with at least one family that seems perpetually lost: the parents who never read the materials sent home, who always seem to "lose" their child's class schedule, who are too overwhelmed with work, school, and sports schedules to make it to Sunday Eucharist as a family. The D.R.E. spends as much time following up with visits and telephone calls to this one family as he or she does in organizing the entire program for the other families; the child's teacher devotes more time helping this unprepared child than with all the other children in the class.

The D.R.E. reaches a point where he or she wants to write them off and move on without them: *Why do they bother if it means so little to them? Why do I bother when they don't care*, the D.R.E. wonders, quite understandably.

But there are those moments when the "lost" are "found": when a child comes to understand—*really* understand—how much God loves that child and every child; when the First

Eucharist or confirmation celebration becomes a moment of conversion for the whole family; when parents come to appreciate what the D.R.E., the teachers, and the parish have done for them. Dealing with the "lost families" is frustrating, aggravating, and, yes, unfair and unjust. But, through the grace of God, they are "found." It is an experience of great joy for the family—and for the D.R.E. and teachers.

We all have "lost" sheep in our lives—well, if not lost, certainly misplaced. They monopolize our attention, usurp our energy, and demand more of our time than they are reasonably entitled to. They anger us, frustrate us, and sometimes even turn on us. But Jesus asks us to "hang tough" with them, not to reject them or move on without them, because everyone is precious and "worth it" in the eyes of God. God throws away no one; God does not write off anyone as hopeless or irredeemable. Such difficult love is but a taste of the limitless mercy of God for all of us. Christ promises us the grace and strength to keep seeking the lost among us and rejoice in their recovery, their conversion, their "being found."

Meditation: Is there a "stray" in your life who demands more from you than you are able to give, who takes advantage of your generosity and sympathy? Can you find within yourself God's grace to continue to seek them out?

Prayer: Gracious God, give us the patience to seek out and bring back the lost and stray sheep in our families and communities. Never let us forget that you always search us out when we are lost in fear and despair; may we possess a measure of that love for those you send us out to bring back.

December 12: Feast of Our Lady of Guadalupe
(Catholic Church)

Wednesday of the Second Week of Advent
(Episcopal Church)

Roses in December

Scripture: Zech 2:14-17 or Rev 11:19a; 12:1-6a, 10ab; Luke 1:26-38 or Luke 1:39-47

Reading:
"And how does this happen to me,
that the mother of my Lord should come to me?
For at the moment the sound of your greeting reached my ears,
the infant in my womb leaped for joy." (Luke 1:43-44)

Reflection: Today we celebrate Juan Diego's vision of the Mother of God, Our Lady of Guadalupe. Walking to the barrio of Tepeyac on a December morning in 1531, the Mestizo laborer is stopped by a beautiful woman dressed in Indian attire. In the hard winter ground, roses blossom at her feet, and she instructs Diego to gather up the flowers and take them to the bishop as a sign of God's providence for the poor and subjugated Aztecs. The story of Our Lady of Guadalupe was an experience of conversion for the young church in the Americas, which transformed itself from the church of the Spanish conquerors to the church of the poor and oppressed.

Roses in December, green boughs of Christmas—signs of life and vibrancy in the midst of the frozen dormancy of winter. But beneath the winter cold, quiet growth is taking place: the soil is being enriched for spring planting; the buds of trees quietly grow and develop foliage that will eventually sprout; flower bulbs are strengthened with nutrients to break through the soil in April; the rain and snow of winter replenish the lakes and streams for the year ahead. Winter is the season of gestation, of preparing, of waiting.

Winter can be a depressing time for us humans—yet it is in winter that we discover the God *within,* the God who dwells in our hearts and who animates our spirits and speaks to our consciences. In the love of family and friends this Christmas, may we behold the light of God's love in the dead of winter; in our generosity and kindness, may we make roses blossom in the December cold; in our struggle to imitate the forgiveness and justice of the gospel, may our lives begin to be transformed in Advent peace.

Meditation: How can you make this Advent winter a time for rediscovering the God *within?* How might you make flowers blossom for someone in the hard winter earth?

Prayer: Gracious God, may your word of life take root in our winter souls that we may experience the warmth and light of your eternal spring. Let your grace melt the coldness of estrangement and despair that grips us. Let your wisdom be the light that illuminates the dark confusion and hopelessness that separate us from you and from one another.

December 13: Memorial of St. Lucy, Virgin and Martyr
(Catholic Church)

Thursday of the Second Week of Advent
(Episcopal Church)

Living Forgiveness

Readings: Isa 41:13-20; Matt 11:11-15

Scripture:

"Amen, I say to you,
among those born of women
there has been none greater than John the Baptist;
yet the least in the Kingdom of heaven is greater than
he . . ." (Matt 11:11)

Reflection: It is horrifying to imagine what happened that morning in October 2006: A deranged milk truck driver stormed into the one-room schoolhouse in an Amish community in Pennsylvania. He shot ten schoolgirls, killing five of them, before turning the gun on himself.

But what was even more stunning was the response of the Amish. Parents of one of the murdered girls personally approached the widow of the shooter to offer their forgiveness. While they would usually refuse the thousands of dollars donated from people across the country to help with their surviving daughters' medical bills, the self-reliant Amish said they would be denying people the blessing that comes from giving if they were to turn away these gifts—but they insisted on establishing a fund for the killer's wife and three children as well. And when the shooter was buried, half of the seventy-five mourners there were Amish.

This tragedy allowed the outside world a rare glimpse at the remarkable values of the Amish. They love their children as much as we love our children, and the deaths of the five girls were devastating to these families. Their hurt was great—but they didn't balance the hurt with hate. As one Amish mother said, perhaps some good might come from this tragedy: "We can tell people about Christ and actually show you in our walk that we forgive . . ."

In their uncompromising living of the gospel values of compassion and forgiveness, the Amish are prophets in the spirit of John, inviting all of us to bring the water of peace to deserts parched by conflict and violence, to plant cedars of compassion in wastelands of injustice and hatred. In giving the needs of others priority over our own interests, in taking the first humbling steps toward reconciliation with another, in seeing in others the face of Christ, we bring the kingdom of God to reality in our own time and place.

Meditation: In what small ways can you imitate that sense of compassion and forgiveness practiced by the Amish?

Prayer: Christ Jesus, help us to seek the greatness of being the least in your Father's kingdom. May we embrace the spirit of humility of your birth and the spirit of servanthood of your selfless giving to all who came to you in their pain and despair.

Grow Up!

Readings: Isa 48:17-19; Matt 11:16-19

Scripture:

"To what shall I compare this generation?
It is like children who sit in marketplaces and call to one another,
'We played the flute for you, but you did not dance,
we sang a dirge but you did not mourn.'" (Matt 11:16-17)

Reflection: Children are exasperating. They live for the moment; they become bored in an instant. More often than not, they have no idea what they want—but are clear about what they *don't* want. Whatever they have, they want something else. They bristle at limits and chafe at rules but are not mature enough to function without them. Children have the innate ability to cajole, to negotiate, to make their parents feel horrible for *daring* to say no.

The truth is that we adults are often like children when it comes to our relationship with God. We want God to do this and mean this one day, then be something entirely different the next day: *Forgive us, O God, but punish those who hurt us. Bless us, but don't let that other guy get more than us. If I'm good today, O God, can I get tomorrow off?*

In today's short parable, Jesus admonishes those whose faith seems to be stuck in childishness. "This generation,"

Jesus says, are like sullen, persnickety children, who reject the austerity of John while at the same time reject the openness of Jesus. They find fault with the "dirge" of repentance played by John and the "flute" of joy played by Jesus. They refuse to play either the "happy" games of Jesus or the "serious" games of John.

Wisdom demands a mature approach to God and the things of God. A maturity of faith is centered in the realization that we are not the center of the universe, that there exists outside of ourselves a sacred entity that breathes life into our beings and animates all of creation. To become an adult person of faith begins with gratitude for the gift of life that is of and from God. The love of God starts with the realization of the needs of another, putting our own wants second. Christ calls us to a child*like* faith of simplicity and humility, not a child*ish* faith of "even-Stevens" and "me-firsts."

Meditation: In what ways can you live your faith in a more mature way?

Prayer: Loving Father, help us to grow in our faith. Do not let us stagnate in an immature, unchallenging relationship with you; lift us up out of our simplistic approach to you and help us to mature as men and women who seek you in all things and gratefully take on the challenges of being your holy people.

A Sermon Never Preached

Readings: Sir 48:1-4, 9-11; Matt 17:9a, 10-13

Scripture:

". . . Elijah will indeed come and restore all things;
but I tell you that Elijah has already come,
and they did not recognize him but did to him whatever they pleased." (Matt 17:11-12)

Reflection: Marilynne Robinson's acclaimed novel *Gilead* is in the form of a long letter from a Congregationalist pastor in his mid-70s to his seven-year-old son. The dying old man wants to tell his son some things that he never had an opportunity to tell him or that his son will be able to appreciate only when he is older.

In the course of his letter, the pastor calculates that if all the sermons he preached were bound in books, they would total 225 volumes, "which puts me up there with Augustine and Calvin for quantity." He is convinced, however, that his best sermon is one he never delivered. He wrote it during World War I when many people in Iowa were dying of influenza. The young men who succumbed to the disease, he wrote, were actually being spared a far worse fate. The Lord "was gathering them in before they could go off and commit murder against their brothers," he wrote then.

While he was convinced of its message, he could not bring himself to deliver the sermon because he knew that the only people who would hear it were the beleaguered folk who were already "sad and apprehensive as they could stand to be and no more approving of the war than I was." One pastor put the sermon aside, aware that it would not be heard in the noise of the conflict.

Sadly, our world needs to hear the Word of God in the fire of Elijah and the passion of John the Baptizer. The justice of God proclaimed by the great prophet Elijah must be restored in our own commitment to what is right and just; the forgiveness preached by John at the Jordan must resonate in our own reconciliation with God and with one another. By virtue of our baptism into the life of Christ, we take on the role of prophet, proclaiming by how we live that the kingdom of God is in our midst. The call to prophesy often demands that we struggle to hear the "sermons" that challenge our self-centered view of the world and to "preach" those values of God that run counter to the dictates of our practical, pragmatic world.

Meditation: What dimension of the Advent Scriptures do you find most difficult to hear and embrace?

Prayer: Make us prophets in our own time and place, O saving God. Ignite in us the fire of Elijah that we may proclaim in our actions your reign of justice and reconciliation. Open our lips to speak the good news of John the Baptist, that in our compassion and humility, we may proclaim your love in our midst.

THIRD WEEK OF ADVENT

True Gifts

Readings: Isa 35:1-6a, 10; Jas 5:7-10; Matt 11:2-11

Scripture:
"Go and tell John what you hear and see:
the blind regain their sight,
the lame walk,
lepers are cleansed,
the deaf hear,
the dead are raised,
and the poor have the good news proclaimed to them."
(Matt 11:4-5)

Reflection: In the midst of Christmas shopping for her children one year, Marian Wright Edelman, president of the Children's Defense Fund, realized that the best presents she received as a child were not wrapped in pretty boxes and found under the Christmas tree. From her father, for example, she had been given her love of reading and learning. From her mother, she received her concern for children without homes and parents unable to care for them. From a neighbor, "Miz Tee," who lived down the street, young Marian was given the gift of courage not to be afraid of anything in life when something important needed to be done. And from her high school teacher, Marian was given an appreciation of her black heritage. Edelman will forever remember the day her teacher arranged for the great poet Langston Hughes to come to her school and meet with her students.

Reflecting on these many gifts, Edelman writes:

> But I carry with me and treasure the lessons in living I was given throughout my childhood by my parents and by concerned and loving community elders. May these memories give me the strength to stop shopping, and instead give a child a true gift— time spent with a caring adult, time spent sharing some of the great lives and spirits of mentors who have enriched, informed and helped shape my life.

Advent challenges our whole attitude and approach to, among other things, our holiday shopping and gift giving. The true gifts of Christmas that Christ gives and enables us to give to one another can transform the hearts and lives of those we love: gifts of teaching, of sharing our time and experience, of compassion and reconciliation, of forgiveness and affirmation.

Meditation: What can you give someone this Christmas that will bring him or her healing, understanding, or comfort?

Prayer: O God, Giver of all good things, make us grace-filled givers this Christmas. Open our hearts to give to others the compassion and peace of Christ that transforms emptiness to wholeness, sadness to joy, death to life.

The Story Begins

Readings: Gen 49:2, 8-10; Matt 1:1-17

Scripture:
The book of the genealogy of Jesus Christ,
the son of David, the son of Abraham. (Matt 1:1)

Reflection: Where does the story of Jesus begin?

If we were telling the story, we would start with the cave at Bethlehem.

But Matthew reminds us that the story of Jesus begins with God—the God who reveals himself to the desert nomad Abraham as the Creator of all things and Sustainer of all that lives, the God who envisions a world where all people are his children and are brothers and sisters to one another. That is where the story of Jesus begins: with the uncompromising, powerful love of God—love that was the force of both creation stories in Genesis.

And so, Matthew begins his gospel with an account of Jesus' ancestry. The historical accuracy of the list is dubious; but that is not the point. The point is this: that this Jesus is the fulfillment of God's vision for a world and a humanity created in the compassion, justice, and peace of its Creator. It is a vision that includes desert nomads and kings, shepherds and farmers, saints and sinners, the powerful and the powerless. It is a vision that transcends geography and culture and status—and even time itself.

As God called Abraham, Judah, Tamar, David, Hezekiah, Eliakem, and Joseph and Mary of the first Advent to prepare for the appearance of Christ, God calls us of the second Advent to prepare for the reappearance of Christ at the fulfillment of time.

Meditation: In what ways has a sense of God's love made a lasting difference in your life?

Prayer: God of all times and seasons, you called generations before us to make ready for the dawning of your Christ. Grateful for the faith we have received from them, help us to pass that faith on to our children and our children's children, that your dream—the kingdom for which your Son lived and died—may be realized in every time and place.

Claimed in Love

Readings: Jer 23:5-8; Matt 1:18-25

Scripture:

"Joseph, son of David,
do not be afraid to take Mary your wife into your home.
For it is through the Holy Spirit
that this child has been conceived in her." (Matt 1:20)

Reflection: As it happened, both had been adopted as infants, so both had a special love and understanding for children without parents. Each hoped to one day make a happy home for some parentless child. After they met and fell in love, they were even more determined to one day give a child the same happy home they had been given by their adoptive parents. They married and had two children of their own; then they decided to look into adopting a baby girl from China. While the son of a Chinese couple will one day be able to take over the family farm, many infant girls in China are given up by parents who cannot afford to care for them.

After many months of negotiations, preparations, and waiting, they received the telephone call to go to China immediately and bring home their daughter. Arriving in China forty-eight hours later, they were taken to a dingy building that served as an orphanage. She reached down into the crib and picked up the child; he gathered them both in his arms and kissed the child on the forehead. They claimed her, in love, as their own. She was now their daughter; they were now her mom and dad.

Just as this couple welcomes this little girl as their own, Joseph is asked by God to welcome the Christ Child as his own. In Matthew's version of Jesus' birth, the whole grand event depends on Joseph, whose life has been turned upside down by the angel's news. If Joseph believes the angel, the story can go on. Joseph accepts the son as his own, not as a matter of biology, but as a matter of love and compassion, of trust and faith. As Barbara Brown Taylor writes, "God's birth requires human partners—a Mary, a Joseph, a you, a me—willing to believe the impossible, willing to claim the scandal, to adopt it and give it our names, accepting the whole sticky mess and rocking it in our arms."

Every one of us is asked by God to welcome Christ into our midst. In the mystery of Christmas, God's "yes" depends on our own "yes."

Meditation: How can you take on the role of Joseph this Christmas in bringing the compassion and forgiveness of God into a difficult and strained situation?

Prayer: O God, may we be inspired by the compassion and devotion of Joseph. In times of crisis and tension, bless our families with the hope of your consolation and forgiveness; in times of joy and discovery, bless us with a spirit of gratitude, never forgetting that you are the Father of us all, the Giver of all that is good.

Tongue-tied

Readings: Judg 13:2-7, 24-25a; Luke 1:5-25

Scripture:

"But now you will be speechless and unable to talk
until the day these things take place,
because you did not believe my words,
which will be fulfilled at their proper time." (Luke 1:20)

Reflection: So what do you say?

You meet someone who has just endured a devastating loss or is going through a terrible time, and you have no idea what to say. You encounter someone who has hurt you or cheated you or spoken badly of you (and you know that they have), and you stumble to find the appropriate thing to say in this awkward situation. You run into someone you used to work with who left the company under less-than-happy circumstances or someone who has been caught in a very embarrassing personal situation, and you are hopelessly tongue-tied.

We've all had moments like that. But most of the time, we actually *do* know what to say; we know exactly the words of healing and reconciliation and compassion that should be said. But we are afraid: afraid that we might add to the other person's hurt, afraid that our words could be misunderstood or misconstrued, afraid of being associated with this outcast. We hesitate to speak the words we want to say—and the other person aches to hear—because we don't have faith in our own sense of compassion and integrity, we don't trust that our words will be perceived as sincere and caring.

The story of Zechariah is also about fear and the inability to trust. Zechariah, a priest of the temple and presumably a man of great faith, cannot believe Gabriel's news that he and his beloved Elizabeth, at their ages, will be the parents of a child. Faced with that overwhelming prospect, Zechariah is terrified. So the angelic messenger takes away Zechariah's ability to speak. Zechariah will regain his speech when all that God has promised comes to pass.

God gives us the grace to speak his word of compassion and peace if we trust in that compassion and peace, if we are willing to pay the price for those words as God has paid the price for those words, if we remain faithful to the God who remains faithful to us. During his nine months of enforced silence, Zechariah came to realize that God's word was not confined to the ancient texts of his faith but alive in his own heart and home. That word is alive in our own hearts, as well, enabling us to speak the love of God despite ourselves.

Meditation: Are there words you hesitate to say that could bring healing and consolation to someone you know?

Prayer: Faithful God, help us to trust in your word of love so that we may not hesitate to speak that word to all we encounter. Untie our tongues and free us from our fears so that others may hear your voice of consolation and forgiveness in our words.

"In the Kitchen"

Readings: Isa 7:10-14; Luke 1:26-38

Scripture:

"The Holy Spirit will come upon you,
and the power of the Most High will overshadow you.
Therefore the child to be born
will be called holy, the Son of God." (Luke 1:35)

Reflection: The gospel of the Annunciation has been a revered subject of artists since the Renaissance. Mary is often depicted as a young woman of great beauty and royal bearing, dressed in silks and brocade; as she is immersed in prayer in her palace-like chamber, the winged Gabriel appears, a magnificent figure surrounded by light. But Benedictine Father Kilian McDonnell, in his poem "In the Kitchen," imagines a much different scene:

Bellini has it wrong.
I was not kneeling
on my satin cushion
quietly at prayer,
head slightly bent.

Painters always
skew the scene,
as though my life
were wrapped in silks,
in temple smells.

Actually I had just
come back from the well,
placing the pitcher on the table
I bumped against the edge,
spilling water on the floor.

As I bent to wipe
it up, there was a light
against the kitchen wall
as though someone had opened
the door to the sun.

Rag in hand,
hair across my face,
I turned to see
who was entering,
unannounced, unasked.

All I saw
was light, white
against the timbers.
I heard a voice
I had never heard.

I heard a greeting,
I was elected,
the Lord was with me,
I pushed back my hair,
stood afraid.

Someone closed the door.
And I dropped the rag.

And so Mary's Child comes to us, often unannounced, into our kitchens and living rooms, our offices and plants, our classrooms and playgrounds. He comes to transform not only human history but also our own personal histories. In him, the compassion of God takes on a human face; in him, our everyday struggles and confusions are transformed in the peace of the Father.

Meditation: Have you ever realized God calling you in the midst of the mundane and the ordinary?

Prayer: Lord God, as Mary put aside her confusion and fears to welcome your Son, may we welcome him into our own lives. May the Christ of Christmas transform our lives into hope and joy in every season of the year; may his presence make holy every moment we live, every space we inhabit.

Moment of Grace

Readings: Cant 2:8-14 or Zeph 3:14-18a; Luke 1:39-45

Scripture:

. . . Elizabeth, filled with the Holy Spirit,
cried out in a loud voice and said,
"Most blessed are you among women,
and blessed is the fruit of your womb." (Luke 1:41-42)

Reflection: Ten years ago, Liam Doyle came into the world with an incomplete heart. He was born without one of the four chambers needed for the muscle to pump blood through his little body. Twice before the age of two little Liam underwent open-heart surgery to rebuild his heart. It was a terrifying ordeal for his mom and dad, Mary and Brian. But Brian Doyle writes in *Leaping: Revelations and Epiphanies* that the family's traumatic experience was also a rare occasion of grace:

> The first operation was terrifying, but it happened so fast and was so necessary and was so soon after the day [Liam] was born with a twin brother that all of us—mother, father, sister, families, friends—staggered through the days and nights too tired and frightened to do anything but lurch into the next hour.
>
> But by the second operation my son was nearly two years old, a stubborn, funny, amiable boy with a crooked gunslinger's grin, and when a doctor carried him down the hall, his

moon-boy face grinning at me as it receded toward awful pain and possible death, I went somewhere dark that frightens me still. It was a cold black country that I hope never to visit again. Yet out of the dark came my wife's hand like a hawk, and I believe, to this hour, that when she touched me I received pure grace. She woke me, saved me, not for the first time, not for the last.

As husbands and wives, as mothers and fathers, as sisters and brothers, God has given us one another to create a safe, welcoming place called family. For most of us, family is the harbor we can always go to when storms batter our lives; family is the shelter we can always run to in times of danger; family is that one special place where we are always welcome, forgiven, and loved. In today's gospel, we witness such a moment of grace within the family of Mary and Elizabeth: love that enables one cousin to put aside her own plight to help the other cousin, compassion that allows the older woman to offer comfort and joy to the younger woman as she struggles to adjust to the changes in her life.

Meditation: Who are the Elizabeths in your family whose selfless love and unconditional support are the very presence of God?

Prayer: God of all times and ages, come and make your dwelling place in our midst. May your love be our house of safety and consolation, may your peace be the table where we gather, may your forgiveness be the hearth that warms us and brings us together.

Song of Liberation

Readings: 1 Sam 1:24-28; Luke 1:46-56

Scripture:
"My soul proclaims the greatness of the Lord;
my spirit rejoices in God my savior." (Luke 1:46)

Reflection: Late in World War II, American and British soldiers were languishing in a war camp deep inside Germany. A high barbed wire fence ran across the center of the camp, isolating the two sets of prisoners. But once a day at noon the British and American chaplains could go to the fence and exchange greetings, always in the company of guards.

The Americans had managed to assemble a wireless radio and were able to hear some news from the outside world. The American chaplain would share a headline or two with his British counterpart in the few moments they had at the fence.

One day the news came over the little radio that the German high command had surrendered and the war was over. None of the Germans knew this, since their communications system had broken down. The American chaplain took the headline to the fence and then lingered to hear the thunderous roar of celebration in the British barracks.

An amazing thing then happened. For the next three days the prisoners celebrated, waving at the German guards—

who still did not know the news—and smiling at the vicious dogs. Then, when they awoke on the fourth day, the guards were nowhere to be seen. They had fled into the surrounding forest, leaving the gate unlocked.

That morning the prisoners walked out as "freed men." But they had really been free four days earlier by the news that the war was over. As the British chaplain later said, "That is the power of the Gospel—it is news, not advice."

In today's gospel, Mary is transformed by the news she first heard from Gabriel and now confirms with her cousin Elizabeth. God's promise of the Messiah fills Mary with hope—hope that enables Mary and Elizabeth to cope with the struggles of their difficult lives and a very uncertain future. Mary's beautiful canticle expresses her hope in God's endless faithfulness and limitless mercy.

We who live in humankind's second Advent now await the return of the Christ of the world to come. That same news should also fill us with hope and a sense of liberation as we slog through life's disappointments, hurts, and broken promises. Our faith in God's promise, as Mary's *Magnificat* celebrates, gives us reason to hope in the midst of bleak despair and to rejoice in the face of overwhelming cynicism.

Meditation: What words in Mary's song of praise most resonate for you this Advent?

Prayer: O God, may Mary's song become our song of joy and hope. May we live our lives in the spirit of the *Magnificat*, lifted up by your grace, humbled by your forgiveness, grateful for the countless good things you have given us.

FOURTH WEEK OF ADVENT

The Scandal of Emmanuel

Readings: Isa 7:10-14; Rom 1:1-7; Matt 1:18-24

Scripture:

The angel of the Lord appeared to him in a dream and said,
"Joseph, son of David,
do not be afraid to take Mary your wife into your home.
For it is through the Holy Spirit
that this child has been conceived in her." (Matt 1:20)

Reflection: Today's gospel is Matthew's version of the annunciation of Jesus' birth. Matthew writes of a young unmarried woman suddenly finding herself pregnant and her hurt and confused husband wondering what to do. In gospel times, marriage was agreed upon by the groom and the bride's parents almost immediately after the age of puberty; but the bride continued to live with her parents after the wedding until the husband was able to support her in his own home or that of his parents. During that interim, marital intercourse was not permitted—yet Mary is found to be with child. Joseph, an observant and compassionate Jew, does not wish to subject Mary to the full fury of Jewish Law, so he plans to "divorce her quietly."

But in images reminiscent of the Old Testament "annunciations" of Isaac and Samuel, an angel appears to Joseph in a dream and reveals that this child is the fulfillment of Isaiah's prophecy. Trusting in God's promise, Joseph acknowledges the child and agrees to name him "Jesus" ("God saves"). Thus Joseph becomes, in the eyes of the Law, the legal father of Jesus. And Jesus, through Joseph, is born a descendant of David; and the fulfillment of Isaiah's prophecy regarding the coming of "Emmanuel" is set in motion.

In Matthew's Gospel, the whole grand event depends on Joseph, whose life has been turned upside down by the angel's news. Joseph puts aside his own confusion and hurt and welcomes the child as his own, not as a matter of biology, but as a matter of love and compassion, of trust and faith. God's birth in our midst depends on men and women with the capacity to love as Joseph does, who are willing to believe the impossible, willing to claim the unwanted, willing to love the helpless and needy, willing to put aside their own fears and dare to hope that God is with us. Every one of us is called to be Joseph—to welcome God in our midst. In the mystery of Christmas, God's "yes" depends on our own "yes."

Meditation: What is the hardest part of Christmas for you?

Prayer: Come, Emmanuel, and make your dwelling place among us. May we welcome you into our midst when your presence is most demanding, inconvenient, and threatening. May we give birth to you despite our doubts and fears, our timidity and weakness.

Preparing the Stable

Readings: 2 Sam 7:1-5, 8b-12, 14a, 16; Luke 1:67-79

Scripture:
"In the tender compassion of our God
the dawn from on high shall break upon us,
to shine on those who dwell in darkness and the shadow of death,
and to guide our feet into the way of peace." (Luke 1:78-79)

Reflection: Barns and stables are fascinating places where every dimension of life and death are played out.

While children find barns exciting places of discovery and wonderful places to play, for farmers and ranchers they are places of hard work, anxiety, and struggle. Within the hard planks of any barn, the new calf is born, young chicks are nurtured, the sick colt is cared for. It is the shelter for animals and the storehouse of the harvest, where hay is stacked, eggs are collected, and cows are milked.

But barns and stables are also filled with the grit and stench that are part of life. They are among the messiest and dirtiest of places. They warehouse old, tired, and useless things—from obsolete tools to irreparably broken vehicles—until they are long forgotten.

And yet, in the Christmas moment, God transforms a cave used as a barn, a stable in a small backwater town, into the holiest of shrines, the most sacred of places.

In so many ways, our lives are stables, filled with every joy and pain and tension and mess necessary for us to grow, to heal and mend, to fulfill our dreams and hopes. The Christ who is born in a Bethlehem stable comes to bring light and life into the stables that are each one of us. In Christ's birth every human heart becomes a sacred place where God is born again and again and again.

This will probably be a busy day as you get ready for tonight and tomorrow. But take a moment in the midst of the day's preparations to remember that Christ comes to make every struggle and joy that takes place in your "stable" an experience of God's compassion. Make a place for the Child of Bethlehem in the Bethlehem of your own heart in these days and in every season of the New Year.

Meditation: What one task will you complete on this busy day before Christmas that can most effectively proclaim the birth of the Christ Child?

Prayer: In the birth of your Son, O God, you have touched human history. May the dawning of Christ illuminate every morning; may his birth re-create every human heart; may his presence among us transform our stables and Bethlehems into holy places of your compassion and peace.

CHRISTMAS AND DAYS WITHIN ITS OCTAVE

"Silent night . . ."

Readings:
VIGIL: Isa 62:1-5; Acts 13:16-17, 22-25; Matt 1:1-25 (or 18-25)
MIDNIGHT: Isa 9:1-6; Titus 2:11-14; Luke 2:1-14
DAWN: Isa 62:11-12; Titus 3:4-7; Luke 2:15-20
DAY: Isa 52:7-10; Heb 1:1-6; John 1:1-18 (or 1:1-5, 9-14)

Scripture:
The angel said to [the shepherds],
"Do not be afraid;
for behold, I proclaim to you good news of great joy
that will be for all the people.
For today in the city of David
a savior has been born for you who is Christ and Lord."
(Luke 2:10-11)

Reflection: *Silent night, holy night, / All is calm, all is bright . . .*
A holy night, to be sure. But hardly silent and anything but calm.

That night in Bethlehem, in a cold, dark manger, a frightened young woman gave birth to her child, amid the cries and howls, the bleating and the braying. Finally, a newborn's first cries for life broke the stillness. This "silent night" was filled with fear, pain, and the exhaustion of childbirth.

There was no "calm" that night in crowded, chaotic Bethlehem, a little hamlet bursting at the seams with visitors and travelers for the great census. There was no "calm" in all of Israel—only tension and conflict between the Jewish people and their Roman occupiers. Palestine of the first century was hardly a place of "heavenly peace"—it was a land torn apart by oppression, persecution, and terror.

"Silent night"? Listen again.

"All is bright"? The darkness of fear and chaos reigned.

"All is calm"? Not that night. Not there.

And yet on this noisy, chaotic, anxious night, Christ was born. Sheltered in a dark hovel the light of Christ dawned. Amid the pain and anguish of a broken people, Christ came with new hope and transforming joy.

In the middle of our own dark nights of pain and anguish, God comes and transforms them into "holy" nights of his peace. Amid the noise and clamor that consume us, the voice of God speaks to us in the "silence" of our hearts. This Christmas night, the compassion of God transforms all of our nights and days in the brightness of "heavenly peace."

Meditation: How can you bring the silence and peace of this day into every day of the year?

Prayer: Father, may the birth of your Son illuminate our nights with the brightness of your love; may the poverty of his birth and life among us enable us to recognize the richness of your mercy; may his coming to us as one of us inspire us to lift up one another in the dignity of being your sons and daughters.

Stephen's "Argument"

Readings: Acts 6:8-10; 7:54-59; Matt 10:17-22

Scripture:
As they were stoning Stephen, he called out
"Lord Jesus, receive my spirit." (Acts 7:59)

Reflection: One of the great humanitarians of our age was Albert Schweitzer, who left a brilliant career as a theologian and musician to study medicine and become a medical missionary in Africa. Doctor Schweitzer received the Nobel Peace Prize for his tireless work in the hospital and community in Lambarene, Gabon. He was often asked why he left his accomplished career in academia to work in one of the most depressed regions of the world. In 1958, just a few years before his death, he wrote, "I decided that I would make my life my argument. I would advocate the things I believed in, in terms of the life I lived and what I did."

For Luke, the chronicler of Acts, Stephen's life is his "argument" for the gospel of Jesus. Chosen as one of the seven deacons, Stephen is committed to the church's works of compassion. Full of "grace and power," Stephen's life parallels that of Jesus: like Jesus, he is known as a worker of wonders and an eloquent preacher; like Jesus, Stephen courageously indicts the Jewish leaders for their hypocrisy and faithlessness; like Jesus, Stephen dies humbly, giving over his spirit to God and asking forgiveness for his killers.

The death of Stephen is a watershed event for the early church. Stephen is the first of the next generation of leaders after the apostles. The young church begins to see its life and identity beyond Judaism, that it was called to embark on a mission that embraced the world beyond Jerusalem.

Stephen is a model for the baptized of every succeeding time and place, those who are called to make their lives an "argument" for Christ. Today's feast of Stephen, the first martyr, reminds us that Christmas leads to the Cross, that the child whose birth is acclaimed by angels is destined for a humiliating death, that the good news he will preach will exact a heavy price. Yet the wonder of the Christ event is the reality that the story of Jesus, the story of Stephen, the story of the prophets and martyrs of every age does not end with their crucifixions and stonings.

Meditation: How can you make some part of your life your "argument" for the gospel of Jesus?

Prayer: God of compassion, fill us with your spirit as you filled your son Stephen. May we imitate the generosity and servanthood of Stephen the deacon; may we be witnesses to the gospel of justice and peace as was Stephen the preacher; may we never hesitate to be healers and reconcilers, as was Stephen the worker of wonders; may we live our lives in your promise of eternity, as did Stephen the martyr.

Pulled by God's Grasp

Readings: 1 John 1:1-4; John 20:1a, 2-8

Scripture:
Mary Magdalene ran and went to Simon Peter
and to the other disciple whom Jesus loved, and told
them,
"They have taken the Lord from the tomb,
and we do not know where they put him." (John 20:2)

Reflection: Today the church celebrates the feast of the apostle John, the reputed author of the Fourth Gospel and the figure traditionally believed to be the "beloved disciple." John, his brother James, and Peter made up Jesus' inner circle. John is present at the transfiguration and the events in Gethsemane; hanging on the cross, Jesus entrusts to John the care of his mother; and John is among the first to grasp what has happened on Easter morning. Today's gospel is John's account of the resurrection.

In the iconography of the Eastern Church, an ancient motif depicts Jesus' descent into hell after his crucifixion. Painted in the earliest days of Christianity, the scene pictures the risen Christ standing on the battered-down doors of hell. He extends his hands to a man and woman, representing Adam and Eve, to take them from the darkness of hell into the light of heaven. Locks and chains, symbols of bondage, float mysteriously in a vast black space below the figures.

But looking closely at the icon, one can see that Christ is not merely affectionately clasping Adam and Eve's hands. Christ *grabs* Adam and Eve by the wrists and forcefully yanks them out of their tombs into the freedom of his resurrection. In some renditions of this icon, the first parents' expressions suggest not only surprise but also confusion—it's almost as if they are not sure they want to be freed from their place in hell.

It is a telling detail. God will not be dissuaded from being reconciled with his beloved creation. In Christ, God takes the initiative in our salvation; God makes the first and last move in our redemption. Compelled by the unfathomable love that is uniquely of God, God humbles himself to become human in order to pull us into eternity.

Meditation: When have you felt the "pull" of God in your life, God "pulling" you toward forgiveness, toward justice, toward transformation?

Prayer: Incarnate God, pull us out of our tombs of despair and doubt and raise us up to the light of hope and compassion. May we return your constant love for us by imitating your initiative in forgiveness and compassion and your unwavering demand for justice and peace for all your sons and daughters.

The Innocent

Readings: 1 John 1:5–2:2; Matt 2:13-18

Scripture:

When Herod realized that he had been deceived by the magi,
he became furious.
He ordered the massacre of all the boys in Bethlehem and its vicinity
two years old and under,
in accordance with the time he had ascertained from the magi. (Matt 2:16)

Reflection: Today the Christmas story takes a bloody turn. The brutal Herod, terrified that his power might be usurped by this "newborn king of the Jews" (Matt 2:2a), orders the massacre of all the boys two years old and younger.

The slaughter of the innocents—this horrifying story has been relived too many times. Our own world has witnessed the suffering and death of the innocent in the wake of unimaginable evil: the extermination of millions of Jews in the Holocaust, the ongoing genocide in Sudan, the victims of 9/11. The innocent die every day as a result of injustice, racism, and selfishness: the young girl killed by a drunk driver, the teenager caught in the crossfire of a gang war, the woman shot for the few dollars in her wallet.

God dies in the death of every innocent who is destroyed by the self-absorbed Herods of our own Palestines; God cries out in the lamentations of every Rachel who mourns for her innocent sons and daughters. In Christ, God calls us to transform the suffering and death of the innocent into God's rule of justice and peace.

Meditation: How can you ease the suffering of the innocent you know? What injustices can you address that will restore justice and mercy to your corner of God's kingdom?

Prayer: God of mercy, open our hearts to hear the cries of the many innocent victims of war, addiction, and abuse. By your grace and their inspiration, may we work to bring comfort and healing, justice and freedom to a world broken and enslaved.

The Night Is Over

Readings: 1 John 2:3-11; Luke 2:22-35

Scripture:

[Simeon] took him into his arms and blessed God, saying:
". . . my own eyes have seen the salvation
which you prepared in the sight of every people,
a light to reveal you to the nations
and the glory of your people Israel." (Luke 2:28-32)

Reflection: An old Indian chief was standing night watch with his young braves. The braves asked the chief how they would know when the night was over and the dawn had broken fully.

"Can we be sure night is over," they asked, "when we can tell the difference between a cow and a sheep on that hill over there?"

"No," said the chief.

"Will we know that the night is over when we can see the color of the bird on the branch of a tall tree?"

"No," he said.

"Well, then," the young braves asked, "how can we know?"

The chief answered, "You will know that the night is over when you look into the face of the man next to you and see your brother."

In the birth of Christ, humanity's long night of sin and death comes to an end; with Simeon, we behold the light that dawns in the birth of this child. He is the Word who breaks down the walls of alienation and estrangement between peoples; he is the peace that bridges the divides between people; he is the light that ends the long night of self-centeredness and despair.

But we also know too well that Simeon's prophecy for Mary and Joseph's son will come to pass. He is the Word who will shake the kingdoms of the proud and powerful; he is the light who will reveal the hypocrisy and shallowness of those who manipulate and use others in the name of God; he is the sign who will contradict the conventional wisdom that places self before the common good, that permits fear to overrule hope, that defines authority in terms of wealth and celebrity instead of moral and ethical integrity.

The challenge of Christmas is to embrace the Christ of the cross with the same joy and hope as we welcome the Child of Bethlehem.

Meditation: At what point in the gospel do we begin to lose interest in Jesus? When do Jesus' words begin to sound too hard, too difficult, too unrealistic to embrace?

Prayer: Christ our light, illuminate our hearts to recognize your presence in one another. May your word dispel the darkness of fear and self-centeredness that enshrouds our world; may our hearts and minds, transformed in your compassion, be reflections of your glory.

DECEMBER 30–JANUARY 5

December 30: Feast of the Holy Family
(Catholic Church)
The Sixth Day in the Octave of Christmas
(Episcopal Church)

A Family Decision

Readings: Sir 3:2-6, 12-14; Col 3:12-21 (or 3:12-17); Matt 2:13-15, 19-23

Scripture:
The angel of the Lord appeared to Joseph in a dream and said,
"Rise, take the child and his mother, flee to Egypt,
and stay there until I tell you.
Herod is going to search for the child to destroy him."
(Matt 2:13)

Reflection: In his book, *All Rivers Run to the Sea,* Elie Wiesel recalls a terrible moment confronting his family. The war was coming to an end, but the deportation of the Jews continued. Elie—who was fifteen at the time—his parents, and three sisters faced deportation to the Nazi concentration camp at Birkenau. Maria, a Christian and the family's housekeeper, begged the Wiesels to hide in her family's cabin in the mountains. The family gathered at the kitchen table for a family meeting: Should they go with Maria or stay and take their chances? The family decided to stay. "A Jew must never be separated from his community," Elie's father said. "What happens to everyone else happens to us as well."

Elie Wiesel writes of their decision: "My father was right. We wanted to stay together, like everyone else. Family unity is one of our important traditions, as the enemy well knew . . . the strength of the family tie, which had contributed to the survival of our people for centuries, became a tool in its exterminator's hands."

Like the Wiesels, the family of Joseph, Mary, and the child Jesus had to endure a great deal as well: the scandal of Mary's pregnancy, Mary's giving birth far from home, their fleeing from Herod's murderous wrath. Yet their love for one another and their trust in God kept their family together through the worst of times.

Every family experiences its share of difficult moments and challenges. Today, on this Sunday after Christmas, we celebrate "family"—that unique nucleus of society that nurtures and supports us throughout our journey on earth. This Christmas season, may we rediscover the special bond that transforms a household into a family—a family that is a harbor of forgiveness and understanding and a safe place of unconditional love, welcome, and acceptance.

Meditation: What has been the hardest situation your family has had to deal with? How were you able to cope with it?

Prayer: Loving Father, in times of tension, bless our family with the hope of your consolation and forgiveness; in times of joy, bless us with a spirit of thankfulness, never letting us forget that you are Father of us all.

The Bandage Changer

Readings: 1 John 2:18-21; John 1:1-18

Scripture:
And the Word became flesh
and made his dwelling among us,
and we saw his glory,
the glory as of the Father's only-begotten Son,
full of grace and truth. (John 1:14)

Reflection: A rabbi prayed to the great prophet Elijah.

"Where," the rabbi asked, "shall I find the Messiah?"

"At the gate of the city," the prophet replied.

"But how shall I recognize him?"

"He sits among the lepers."

"Among the lepers!" the rabbi cried. "What is the Messiah doing there?"

"He changes their bandages," Elijah replied. "He changes their bandages one by one."

"The Word became flesh and made his dwelling among us," reads the Prologue of John's Gospel. The phrase "made his dwelling among us," however, is more accurately translated as "pitched his tent among us." That beautifully expresses the true mystery of Christmas: that in becoming one of us, God "pitched his tent" among ours, lived among us and lived through our moments of joy, grief, despair, anger, and fear. Christ is the Word of God with a human face, the embodiment of the very love of God—love present in the compassion and forgiveness we extend to one another; love present in our efforts to carry on his work of reconciliation and peace; love present in our care to "change the bandages of the lepers" at our gates, "one by one."

Meditation: In what everyday experiences are you most aware that God has "pitched his tent" in your midst, that God is present "changing the bandages" of the "lepers" at your gates?

Prayer: Christ Jesus, you are the word that sets all of creation into motion; you are the light that illuminates every human life; you are the love of God in flesh and blood. Let your Word echo in our hearts that we may re-create the world in the Father's compassion; let your light shatter the darkness of sin and alienation; let your love be the glory we seek, imitating your example of humble and grateful service to one another.

January 1: Solemnity of Mary, Mother of God
(Catholic Church)

The Holy Name
(Episcopal Church)

To Give Birth to God

Readings: Num 6:22-27; Gal 4:4-7; Luke 2:16-21

Scripture:
And Mary kept all these things
reflecting on them in her heart. . . .
When eight days were completed for his circumcision,
he was named Jesus, the name given him by the angel
before he was conceived in the womb. (Luke 2:19, 21)

Reflection: Ever since she saw her mother try on the gloves in the department store, the ten-year-old girl decided she would buy them for her mother as a Christmas present. For weeks, she put aside part of her allowance; she earned extra money doing chores and running errands for neighbors. On Christmas morning, she saw the delight on her mother's face as she opened the box. In the joy she experienced by bringing joy to her mom, God was born.

A group of volunteers from a local church have spent the past dozen weekends at the building site. Under the direction of professional carpenters and tradespeople who have donated their time as well, they framed the house, hung the sheet rock, painted and tiled, and are now completing the finishing work. Whether they realize it or not, they are building more than a house for a family in need: they are making a dwelling place for God.

One night a week, she returns to her classroom at the local high school. Her students are not teenagers but adults who never finished high school and immigrants from Latin America and Asia. Together they struggle through vocabulary, spelling, and literature. With each new word understood and passage grasped, this young teacher gives birth—to God.

The great Dominican theologian Meister Eckhart preached "we are all meant to be mothers of God" for "God is always needing to be born." God seeks to be born in our own loveless stables and forgotten caves; God waits to come to life in our Bethlehems of anger, estrangement, and hopelessness; God makes a dwelling place for himself in the Nazareths of our homes, schools, and workplaces.

On this first day of the New Year, we honor Mary, the Mother of God, under her most ancient title, that of *Theotokos*, the Greek word for "bearer of God." In baptism into the life of Mary's child, we are called to be "bearers of God"—to give birth to God, to be transformed in God's light and love.

Meditation: In what real, concrete ways can you give "birth" to God in the year ahead?

Prayer: Gracious God, in your gift of this New Year may we create a dwelling place for you in our works of charity and reconciliation. May we give birth to you in every word of consolation and support we speak, in every joy we bring into the lives of others.

Discovering God Within

Readings: 1 John 2:22-28; John 1:19-28

Scripture:
John answered [the Pharisees]:
"I baptize with water;
but there is one among you whom you do not recognize,
the one who is coming after me,
whose sandal strap I am not worthy to untie." (John 1:26-27)

Reflection: The congregation was very proud of their beautiful church, which had stood proudly on the New England village common for generations. But one night just before Thanksgiving, a spark in the heating system ignited a fire that destroyed the clapboard structure. Fortunately, no one was hurt, but the congregation was devastated. As soon as the fire marshal gave the all clear, the stunned pastor and parishioners combed the rubble to salvage the few things they could.

Then, interesting things began to happen.

A nearby church—a congregation the displaced church had little to do with before—offered them the use of their religious education building for services and meetings. Churches from nearby towns offered hymnals and other supplies; several churches took up a collection for the congregation.

At the first service following the fire, the congregation, who were used to sitting in their "own" places at a comfortable distance from one another, found themselves sitting side by side on folding chairs. After the service, teams started to form to deal with insurance, to make temporary arrangements for religious education, and to develop plans for a new church. Parishioners who knew one another only by name and had exchanged only pleasant but perfunctory hellos on Sundays were now working together to rebuild not just their beautiful building but also the community they had taken for granted.

And in their grief and loss that first Sunday morning in their temporary quarters, they prayed and sang in a way few had ever experienced before. In the new journey they had begun as a church, they had rediscovered the God within them.

In today's gospel, John the Baptist challenges the Pharisees to realize what this congregation understood anew after the loss of their building: that God is among us. This season of Christmas and Epiphany invites us to rediscover God in our midst. Every act of generosity, every effort at healing and reconciliation, every offer of comfort and compassion reveals the presence of the risen Christ in our midst.

Meditation: In what events and circumstances in your life have you been surprised to find God in your midst?

Prayer: Open our senses to recognize you among us, Christ. May we behold you in the love of family and friends; may we reveal your presence in our compassion and generosity.

Things Will Never Be the Same . . .

Readings: 1 John 2:29–3:6; John 1:29-34

Scripture:
John the Baptist saw Jesus coming toward him and said, "Behold, the Lamb of God, who takes away the sin of the world." (John 1:29)

Reflection: Late one night, he and his father took the telescope to a field far away from the lights of the city. His dad carefully set up and positioned the lens. Then Dad had him look down into the eyepiece. What the boy saw filled him with awe. He could see the rings of Saturn, the red craters of Mars, the Sea of Tranquility on Earth's moon. His dad pointed out Polaris, Sirius, the stars of the Big Dipper, Orion, and Andromeda. That night they could also see the lights of the Space Shuttle fly overhead. So began one boy's love of astronomy and fascination with the reaches of outer space. After that night with his dad, he never looked at the stars the same way again.

For years she had listened to the Metropolitan Opera on her radio. Then, for her birthday, her children gave her a trip to New York City and tickets for the Metropolitan's production of Puccini's *Tosca.* With excitement and a little disbelief, she found herself sitting in the majestic hall at Lincoln Center; she was soon transported by the magnificent music and spectacle. Since that wonderful night at the Met, she now hears music with a joy and insight she never knew before.

He always loved to draw. His sketchbook was his retreat, a place that was his alone to enjoy his art. One day an artist friend happened to see his sketches. She recognized a talent in those pages and encouraged him to develop it. She offered suggestions on technique and style—and he soaked it up like a sponge. He enrolled in a watercolor course at the local art institute. His artist friend continued to encourage him and suggested books and exhibits he should see. With a new understanding of form and color, of light and perspective, he sees the world these days with very different eyes.

In today's gospel, John the Baptizer invites us to "behold" the Christ, Jesus, the Word of God made flesh. After meeting the Jesus of the gospels, we will never see the world the same way again; after hearing Jesus' gospel, peace, forgiveness, and justice are possible in ways we couldn't imagine; after seeing the world through Jesus' eyes, our perspectives and attitudes are transformed in his light. Christ is forever in our midst—and to behold that presence changes everything.

Meditation: Where have you encountered Jesus in the most unexpected time or place?

Prayer: Jesus, Lamb of God, may we "behold" your presence in our midst in every moment of this New Year. May your Spirit transform our vision, our perspective, our expectations for this life and the life to come.

Revelations

Readings: 1 John 3:7-10; John 1:35-42

Scripture:

Jesus turned and saw them following him and said to them,
"What are you looking for?"
They said to him, "Rabbi" (which translated means Teacher),
"where are you staying?"
He said to them, "Come, and you will see." (John 1:38-39)

Reflection: It may have happened in a chemistry lab or a writing class or an economics seminar. Or at your first guitar lesson or when your grandfather taught you how to cast a fly rod.

The moment you first saw a living cell under a microscope, the cosmos became an exciting place of wonder and discovery.

The first time you were able to strum three chords in succession, your life had a soundtrack.

The first time you cast a fly on a brook in springtime under the watchful eye of grandpa, you embarked on a lifelong friendship with nature.

After the writing instructor showed you how to structure sentences and paragraphs to create moods, heighten suspense, or make readers laugh, you never wrote—or read—a story the same way again.

We have all had those moments, some funny, some painful, when our spouses, our children, our friends showed us something about ourselves that we never realized before—and, as a result, our lives were never the same.

We have all had the experience of learning something we didn't know, of coming to a new understanding of some concept or idea, of having our eyes opened to the different, the possible, the transforming—and we have never looked at our world the same way again.

Just as Andrew and Simon and the disciples discovered when they met Jesus, we also discover that encountering Jesus means we will never again see the world in the same way. Christ is forever in our midst—and to behold that presence changes everything.

Meditation: How does faith affect your perspective as you struggle to deal with a difficult or confounding situation in your life?

Prayer: Compassionate God, may the presence of Christ in our midst transform our perspectives and attitudes. In "beholding" his presence in the word of the gospel and the sacrament of the Eucharist, may we transform our lives and our world from sin to selflessness, from despair to purpose, from death to life.

God in Unexpected Places

Readings: 1 John 3:11-21; John 1:43-51

Scripture:
Philip found Nathanael and told him,
"We have found the one about whom Moses wrote in the law,
and also the prophets, Jesus, son of Joseph, from Nazareth."
But Nathanael said to him,
"Can anything good come from Nazareth?"
Philip said to him, "Come and see." (John 1:45-46)

Reflection: You can't help but hear the sneer in Nathanael's voice in today's gospel. When Philip invites his friend to come and meet Jesus, Nathanael, reflecting the prevailing belief of the time that one's social status was dependent on place of birth, caustically replies, "Can anything good come from Nazareth?"

Come on, Phil! Nazareth? That backwater? It's a couple of farms in the middle of nowhere*! There's nothing there, Phil, NOTHING!*

If we learn anything from the Christmas gospels, it is that God can be found in the most unexpected of places. God is present in the poverty and turmoil of our own Nazareths. God reveals himself in the generosity of a volunteer worker in a soup kitchen, in the patience of a teacher tutoring a struggling student, in the understanding of a high school senior who befriends the kid nobody else has time for. God's peace transforms our most challenging moments into occasions of grace; God's compassion illuminates our darkest nights with hope and a sense of direction.

Whatever Nathanael-like skepticism, biases, and judgments we possess are shattered in the light of Christmas. The dawning of God's Christ calls us to embrace the love Joseph and Mary had for each other that enabled them to endure the many trials of their journey to Bethlehem and the escape to Egypt; to embrace the faith of the shepherds, discovering again and again God's grace in the caves of our despair and want; to embrace the perseverance of the Magi that compels us to seek God in every moment and step of our life's journey.

Often to our surprise, God seeks us in our isolation and invites us to come and realize a life transformed in his Christ.

Meditation: Where and when have you unexpectedly found God?

Prayer: May the light of your grace illuminate our hearts, O God of compassion, dispelling the darkness of skepticism and cynicism, and opening our hearts to behold you in the most unexpected places. Open our eyes and hearts to behold your presence in every place, every moment, and every heart.

EPIPHANY AND BAPTISM OF THE LORD

Sand and Stars

Readings: Isa 60:1-6; Eph 3:2-3a, 5-6; Matt 2:1-12

Scripture:

. . . magi from the east arrived in Jerusalem, saying,
"Where is the newborn king of the Jews?
We saw his star at its rising
and have come to do him homage." (Matt 2:1-2)

Reflection: In December 1954, Carlo Carretto left his life as a successful teacher and renowned writer and activist in Italy and set out for the Algerian Sahara to become a Little Brother of Jesus. He wrote about his ten-year pilgrimage in the African desert in his book *Letters from the Desert:*

> The first nights I spent here made me send off for books on astronomy and maps of the sky; and for months afterwards I spent my free time learning a little of what was passing over my head up there in the universe. . . .
>
> Kneeling on the sand, I sank my eyes for hours and hours in those wonders, writing down my discoveries in an exercise book like a child. . . . Finding one's way in the desert is much easier by night than by day, that the points of reference are numerous and certain. In the years which I spent in the open desert I never once got lost, thanks to the stars. Many times . . . I lost my way because the sun was too high in the

sky. But I waited for night and found the road again, guided by the stars.

We are all stargazers and searchers of one kind or another: some of us seek love and belonging in our lives; others of us follow stars that we hope will lead to wealth, fame, or power. But the Magi and Brother Carlo set their sights on a different star that leads them to God. Their sightings inspire them on journeys of faith, journeys of discovery at the wonder of this gift of life and the Giver of life. The Epiphany—from the Greek word for *appearance* or *manifestation*—calls us to set our sights on the "star" of God that leads us to the joy and lasting treasures of the Christ in our midst.

Meditation: What are the stars that you follow in your life—what "signs" do you find yourself paying the most attention to? Where are they taking you? Is it time to rechart your course?

Prayer: O Christ, the very manifestation of God's love and the radiance of the Father's light, illuminate the path we take on our journey to God. May we come to your Father's dwelling place bearing the most precious gifts we possess: hearts transformed in your love, lives given over to your justice and reconciliation, spirits cast in your peace.

Welcome to the Sandbox

Readings: 1 John 3:22–4:6; Matt 4:12-17, 23-25

Scripture:

[Jesus] went around all of Galilee,
teaching in their synagogues, proclaiming the Gospel of the Kingdom,
and curing every disease and illness among the people. (Matt 4:23)

Reflection: Mikey is having a bad day—as bad a day as a six-year-old can have. There was the paint he knocked over running in school, the punch he threw at his annoying little sister who kept bugging him while he was playing on the computer, and the meatloaf sandwich he wanted no part of at lunch. And now, on this particular afternoon, there was nobody around to play with. So Mikey found himself exiled to the sandbox, mindlessly pushing his prized toy dump truck through the dirt.

After a while, he saw his dad come around the corner. Mom must have told him about the day's misadventures. Mikey didn't look up, he didn't say a word. He just kept pushing his truck through the sand—and steeled himself for the worst.

When Dad got to the edge of the sandbox, he bent down and sat next to Mikey. He took a pail, filled it with sand, and carefully turned it over at one end of the rut Mikey had cut through the sand. Dad then made another perfect mound of sand, and then another. Mikey smiled for the first time all day. For the next hour or two, Mikey and his dad transformed the sandbox into an elaborate network of roads and bridges.

Like Mikey's dad, Jesus gets into the "sandbox" with us. In him, *Emmanuel*—God's being-with-us—included God walking the roads we walk, dealing with the same messy, frustrating problems we deal with, finding joy in the same small experiences in which we find joy. The wonder of the Incarnation is not what God gives up but rather what God takes on: *us*. God shows us that we are not just the object of his work; *we* are his work. We are not just witnesses of his glory; *we* are his glory. In Christ, we are all in the sandbox together. With Christ, we can transform our lives from darkness to light, we can re-create our world from sinful selfishness to hope-filled community.

Meditation: When and how have you experienced Christ's presence in your "sandbox" when you felt alone, rejected, and isolated from others?

Prayer: Christ the Teacher, be the light that illuminates our path as we struggle through the darkness of fear and despair. Christ the Healer, be the salve that eases our pain and mends our wounds from life's hurts and disappointments.

The Four Verbs

Readings: 1 John 4:7-10; Mark 6:34-44

Scripture:
Then, taking the five loaves and the two fish and looking up to heaven,
he said the blessing, broke the loaves, and gave them to his disciples
to set before the people. (Mark 6:41)

Reflection: She had just retired after forty years in the classroom. After a year of traveling, gardening, and reading, she found that she missed the kids. So she volunteered to tutor a couple afternoons a week. One student was having a particularly hard time with equations. She worked with the student after school and, together, they struggled through the mystery of mathematics. Nothing made her happier than when the student received an A on his next math test.

A missionary priest would often write to his friends back home, telling them about the wonderful people in his parish and their struggles. His friends, in turn, set up a fund and crisis money to build a new well for his parish, stock the clinic and school with supplies, and take care of repairs on the mission's buildings. He is grateful for their help; his friends are honored to be part of such holy work.

Every summer the counselors stay a few extra days for the annual "Special Kids' Camp." Even after the long summer, many of the college students happily give their time to provide a camping experience for kids with all kinds of mental and physical challenges. It is the best summer of the kids' lives. It's a demanding weekend and, come Sunday, the counselors are exhausted—but they will be the first to tell you that it's the best part of their summer.

The feeding of the crowd with five loaves of bread and two fish was especially cherished by the early church. They saw Jesus' feeding of the multitude as a precursor to the eucharistic banquet that would bind them—and binds us—into the church of the Risen One. But we, too, can perform wonders in our own time and place by imitating those four decisive eucharistic verbs: *take, bless, break, give—taking* from what we have, *blessing* it by offering it to others in the spirit of God's love, *breaking* it from our own needs and interests for the sake of others, and *giving* it with joy-filled gratitude to the God who has blessed us with so much. By acting on the four verbs of the Eucharist in our everyday lives, we become what we receive in the sacrament of the Body and Blood of the Lord.

Meditation: What can you *take, bless, break,* and *give* today that mirrors the eucharistic action of Jesus?

Prayer: As you give to us, O God, may we give to one another. As Christ takes, blesses, breaks, and gives his body to us in the Eucharist, may we take, bless, break, and give from our own need and so become Eucharist for others.

Catching Melinda

Readings: 1 John 4:11-18; Mark 6:45-52

Scripture:
But when they saw [Jesus] walking on the sea,
they thought it was a ghost and cried out.
They had all seen him and were terrified.
But at once he spoke with them,
"Take courage, it is I, do not be afraid!" (Mark 6:49-50)

Reflection: The day had come. Melinda, all of four and one-half, faced the biggest challenge of her young life: Today, the training wheels would come off of her bicycle.

After detaching the little wheels from the back tire, Dad helped Melinda onto the bicycle and held it—and her—steady. He showed her how to balance herself. As she began to pedal, Dad ran alongside, holding on to the back of the seat. At one point, he let go and Melinda was on her own—for all of ten seconds. Almost immediately she started to lose her balance and fall. "Daddy!" she screamed. Daddy was right there and caught her.

Dad got her set again and, after some encouraging Dad-like words, Melinda was off again. She was doing fine until her foot slipped off the pedal. But Dad was right there again, catching her and the bike.

A third time, with new determination, Melinda got on the bike. Dad ran alongside and when she was going at a pretty good clip, he let go. Melinda was on her way.

And Dad cheered his daughter on as she happily circled the street on her two-wheeler. Victory!

From new bicycles to new schools, from struggling through broken relationships to embarking on the journey of marriage, growing up can be a terrifying experience. But as Melinda's dad was there for her, Jesus promises that, in every storm we face, his hand is extended to us in the hands of those we love and trust. Despite the storms that batter our boats as we make our way across the stormy sea, Christ promises to be that calming presence, that steadying hand, if we keep faith in Christ, who is both our guiding star and our destination.

Meditation: When have you experienced Christ calming a storm in your life in the compassion and support offered by another? When have you been the calming presence of Christ's peace for someone else?

Prayer: May we be your outstretched hand to one another, O Lord. In embracing your spirit of peace and forgiveness, may we create in our homes and churches, our schools and businesses, safe harbors of understanding and support for those struggling to keep their heads above the waters of life's turbulent seas. In seeking to mirror your attitude of humility and selflessness, may we be a lifeline of support and trust for all who cry out to us for help.

Golda

Readings: 1 John 4:19–5:4; Luke 4:14-22

Scripture:

[Jesus] unrolled the scroll and found the passage where it was written:

The Spirit of the Lord is upon me,
because he has anointed me
to bring glad tidings to the poor . . .

He said to them,

"Today this Scripture passage is fulfilled in your hearing." (Luke 4:17-18, 21)

Reflection: The late Dr. Elizabeth Kubler-Ross recounted the story of a young woman she met. Golda was a young Jewish girl living in Germany during the Nazi horror. Her father, mother, brother, and sister perished in the Holocaust. Golda herself escaped death only because she was the last one in line to enter a gas chamber at Maidenak, and the guards couldn't squeeze her in.

When Maidenak was liberated, all Golda wanted was to avenge the death of her family. "But it struck me," Golda said, "that I would be no better than Hitler himself." So Golda went to work in a hospital for children in the town of Maidenak. She had deliberately chosen to help German children—most of them victims of the war like herself—to purge her bitterness toward the German people. And she would remain in Maidenak until she had completely forgiven Hitler.

"When I can do that, then I am allowed to leave."

Golda was an extraordinary prophet in an extraordinary set of circumstances—her sense of forgiveness and sacrifice for the sake of reconciliation is heroic. In our own less-than-extraordinary situations, we are also called by God to be prophets. Embracing the role of prophet begins with the integrity to confront who we are with all our shortcomings, the wisdom to realize the gulf that often exists between the values we profess and the choices we make, and the courage to change and re-create our place in the world in the justice and mercy of God.

Throughout Scripture, the people whom Jesus and the prophets challenge are unable to grasp or accept God's message to change the evil systems that dehumanize the oppressed. In our own simple, everyday lives, may we be prophets who reveal the love of God in our love of others, who give witness to God's forgiveness in our own struggle to forgive and be reconciled with others.

Meditation: Who do you consider to be a prophet in your midst, an individual whose life mirrors Isaiah's prophecy of God's anointed?

Prayer: May your Spirit come upon us, O God, that we may help others see your presence, that we may bring hope and healing to broken relationships and old hurts, that we may be freed from all that impedes our search for you.

"A world larger than your heart"

Readings: 1 John 5:5-13; Luke 5:12-16

Scripture:

[The leper] fell prostrate, pleaded with [Jesus], and said,
"Lord, if you wish, you can make me clean."
Jesus stretched out his hand, touched him, and said,
"I do will it. Be made clean." (Luke 5:12-13)

Reflection: In John Drinkwater's play *Abraham Lincoln,* this exchange takes place between President Lincoln and a Mrs. Blow, a Northerner and anti-Confederate zealot:

Lincoln tells her about the latest victory by Northern forces—the Confederate army lost 2,700 men, while Union forces lost 800. Mrs. Blow is ecstatic. "How splendid, Mr. President!"

Lincoln is stunned by her reaction. "But, madam, 3,500 human lives lost . . ."

"Oh, you must not talk like that, Mr. President. There were only 800 that mattered."

Lincoln's shoulders drop as he says slowly and emotionally: "Madam, the world is larger than your heart."

Our attitudes and perceptions, our vision of the world, often reduce others to "lepers"—those whose beliefs and culture terrify us, those who don't fit our image of sophistication and correctness, those whose religion or race or identity or beliefs seem to threaten our own. We exile these lepers to the margins of society outside our gates; we reduce them to simplistic labels and stereotypes; we reject them as too "unclean" to be part of our lives and our world. The Christ who heals lepers comes to perform a much greater miracle—to heal *us* of our debilitating sense of self that fails to realize the sacredness and dignity of those we demean as "lepers" at our own gates.

Meditation: Who are the "lepers" in your town and village? What makes them "lepers," causing others to shun and reject them? What can you do to help remove the stigma that has been imposed on them?

Prayer: Father of compassion, heal us of our own blindness that prevents us from seeing one another as your children; break through the hardness of our hearts that prevents us from embracing one another as brothers and sisters. May we speak Jesus' word and extend his hand to one another in order to clean and be cleaned of the leprosy of arrogance, pride, and hatred.

That Great Teacher

Readings: 1 John 5:14-21; John 3:22-30

Scripture:
[John said:]
"The one who has the bride is the bridegroom;
the best man, who stands and listens for him,
rejoices greatly at the bridegroom's voice.
So this joy of mine has been made complete.
He must increase; I must decrease." (John 3:29-30)

Reflection: Most of us have had a favorite teacher in school or a professor in college who became more than an instructor—he or she became a trusted mentor and friend. That teacher had the unique ability to make students genuinely excited about learning. You came to share that teacher's passion for science, history, or literature. His or her guidance may have even launched you on your career path and served as a sounding board for you beyond your classroom days. In that teacher's classroom, grades were never the issue, staying awake was never a problem, learning was never drudgery. Such a teacher's love of learning was infectious; there was no limit to that teacher's giving of time and attention to help you discover your own potential and guide you in new and exciting directions.

John the Baptist is like that great teacher. John is completely dedicated to showing others the way to Jesus the "Lamb of God"; his joy is in helping others discover the presence of God in their midst. As John happily "decreases" so that Christ may "increase," as that favorite teacher taught and inspired you, we are invited to teach others about all that God has done for us and help them realize their own gifts and potential to be great. Like the humble baptizer and our generous professor, we are called to testify to the Messiah in our midst by embracing his spirit of humility and selflessness, by living his gospel of reconciliation, justice, and peace.

Meditation: In what unobtrusive, quiet ways can you point out the presence of the "Lamb of God" in the midst of your family and friends?

Prayer: Help us to be inspiring and selfless teachers of your Word, O God, by our committed and joyful embracing of the life and spirit of your gospel. May every act of generosity and selflessness joyfully point to the coming of the Bridegroom into our lives.

Roots: The Naming Rite

Readings: Isa 42:1-4, 6-7; Acts 10:34-38; Matt 3:13-17

Scripture:
After Jesus was baptized,
he came up from the water and behold,
the heavens were opened for him,
and he saw the Spirit of God descending like a dove
and coming upon him.
And a voice came from the heavens, saying,
"This is my beloved Son, with whom I am well
pleased." (Matt 3:16-17)

Reflection: In his landmark novel *Roots,* Alex Haley chronicles his family's history across seven generations, beginning with his ancestor Kunta Kinte who was captured from his village in Gambia and sold into slavery in America.

The story begins with the African naming ceremony that takes place eight days after Kunta Kinte's birth. The name is both a gift and a challenge: the entire village comes together to pray that God will give the child a long life and success in bringing respect, pride, and many children to his family, his village, his tribe. Finally, they pray that he will have the strength and the spirit to bring honor to his name.

Haley describes the gathering of the tribe at which Omoro gives his firstborn son the name *Kunta:*

> [Omoro] lifted up the infant and as all watched, whispered three times into his son's ear the name he had chosen for him. It was the first time the name had ever been spoken as this child's name, for Omoro's people felt that each human being should be the first to know who he was . . .

Out under the moon and stars, Omoro completed the naming ritual. Carrying little Kunta in his strong arms, he lifted him up with his face to the heavens and said softly to him: "Fend kiling dorong leh warrata ka iteh tee" (Behold, the only thing greater than yourself!).

Today's feast of the Baptism of the Lord calls us to remember our own baptisms, our own "naming rites." In baptism, we become part of the "only thing" that is greater than ourselves: the love of God. The same Spirit that descended on Christ at the Jordan descended on us as we were raised up from the waters of the sacrament; and that Spirit continues to dwell in us, leading us and prompting us in the ways of the God who summons us to a life beyond ourselves.

Meditation: In what situations have you felt the Spirit of God prompting you toward a different course of action?

Prayer: Raise us up out of the waters of our baptism, O God, and send your Spirit to dwell in our hearts. May we always be aware that your love is a power greater than anything we possess on our own; may our struggle to live faithfully the gospel of your beloved Son make us worthy of our baptismal name *Christian.*

Acknowledgments

Introduction: Excerpt from Jean Danielou, *The Advent of Salvation* (Glen Rock, N.J.: Deus Books/Paulist Press, 1962), 118.

Dec. 2: Excerpt from Joan Didion, *The Year of Magical Thinking* (New York: Alfred A. Knopf, 2005), 96–97.

Dec 4: Excerpt from Father Henry Fehren, "What Does the Rabbi See?" *U.S. Catholic* (August 1987).

Dec 13: Excerpt from Ann Curry, "Incredible forgiveness." MSNBC (October 4, 2006). http://www.msnbc.msn.com/id/15134112/.

Dec 15: Excerpt from Marilynne Robinson, *Gilead* (New York: Farrar, Straus and Giroux, 2004), 41–43.

Dec 16: Excerpt from Marian Wright Edelman, "The Nature of True Giving." *Christian Science Monitor* (December 22, 1999).

Dec 18: Excerpt from Barbara Brown Taylor, *Gospel Medicine* (Cambridge, MA: Cowley Publications, 1995), 155.

Dec 20: Kilian McDonnell, O.S.B., "In the Kitchen," in *Swift Lord, You Are Not* (Collegeville, MN: Liturgical Press, 2003), 46–47. Reprinted with permission.

Dec 21: Excerpt from Brian Doyle, *Leaping: Revelations and Epiphanies* (Chicago: Loyola Press, 2003), 35–36.

Dec 22: Excerpt from Bill O'Brien, "The Blame Game." *Christian Century* (June 28, 2005). Copyright 2005 Christian Century. Reprinted with permission from the Christian

Century. Subscriptions: $49/yr. from P.O. Box 378, Mt. Morris, IL 61054. 1-800-208-4097.

Dec 26: *Reverence for Life: The Words of Albert Schweitzer,* compiled by Harold E. Robles (San Francisco: HarperSanFrancisco, 1993), 41.

Dec 30: Excerpt from Elie Wiesel, *All Rivers Run to the Sea: Memoirs* (New York: Alfred A. Knopf, 1996), 70.

Jan 6: Excerpt from Carlo Carretto, *Letters from the Desert* (Maryknoll, N.Y.: Orbis Books, 1972), 138–39.

Jan 10: Excerpt from Dr. Elizabeth Kubler-Ross, cited by Christopher Phillips, "To Be Whole Again." *Parade* Magazine (August 11, 1991).

Jan 11: Excerpt from John Drinkwater, *Abraham Lincoln: A Play,* scene three.

Jan 13: Excerpt from Alex Haley, *Roots* (Garden City, N.Y.: Doubleday, 1976), 2–3.